poems

by yousef alqamoussi

Published by Crown Press LLC.
Detroit, Michigan

Cover illustration and design © by Nada Hassan.

ISBN 978-1-79074-7375

Library of Congress Control Number: 2018915137

10 9 8 7 6 5 4 3 2 1

Printed in the United States of America.

poems

WRITTEN

I used to think
that writing is written to be read;
it isn't.
Writing is written
to be written.

HIDE

When it's all too stupid out here,
I hide in books.

DOOR

There is nothing
    quite like
     a locked
        door.

STORIES

"Stories shouldn't end this way," she
  said;
"Stories should end happy and neat
and the good guys should win and evil
  should perish
and
and
and
no mother should have to bury her
  child!"

ALONE

I am
Most
Alone
Among people.

TOXIC

They come in gagging
then spill it onto your lap like heavy
    paint;
how long before you'll get it off?

LONELINESS

It is a wide and gaping hole
that grows within my silent breast
until it has consumed me whole.

TEEN

Janine the Teen
googled "what is deepthroat"
and cried silently alone.

PHONE

I can't seem to find my phone this
    morning
and
that scares the hell outta me.

POSTS

Are you sharing these posts to convince
US?
or to convince yourself?

GUY

Don't judge him so harshly;
he's just a poor sad motherfucker
trying to be happy.

PARTY

You know what is funny.
I invited 15 people.
14 cancelled
lol

SOIRÉE

Eight friends in a room
sipping drinks and laughing with
  nothing to say
is a real hoot.

IMPORTANT

Some of you
must really enjoy feeling important
without being important,
because being important would suck.

MASERATI

To the sixth in line at the Tim Hortons
  drive-thru:
return the Maserati,
buy better coffee.

PURGE

Purge the town
of winners and leaders,
mutant mansions, bedazzled speed-
  rockets
in the streets,
sparkling suits and headgear sheen,
pasty licentious smiles and poster
  lawns,
stale smoke spite and skin
and let us live in peace.

GOLF

The Battle of Patrician was fought on a
  golf course
where bodies strew the tees and sand
  pits;
slaughter smeared the fairways
and wails rang from beneath the toppled
  carts;
heads rolled down the green
and well I suppose that's what happens
  to golf courses.

AD-FREE

"The next thirty minutes of music are
ad-free
thanks to the following sponsor:"

CELEBRATE

Why must I
in order to drop off my Bukowski book
  at the public library
have to cross such a long flowery stony
  sprawling memorial
which celebrates war?

Commemorates

SCROLLINGSLOTSSCROLLING

Scrollingslotsscrollingscrollingscrolli
   ngscrollingscrollingscrol
ad
scrollingscrollingscrollingsc
ad
scrollingscrollingscrollingslotsscrolli
ad
scr
ad
scro
ad
ad ad
adad
dada
scrollingscrollingsclorngiscorlsncirolo
   rocsing.

EGO

Ego

is the
only
evil.

ENLIGHTENMENT

Sit down
shut up
just watch.

DO

If you sit and do nothing,
real things will happen.

TAO

What
Would
Water
Do
?

ZEN

Trees
Clouds
Streams
Are
So
Be.

GOOD

Doing bad ,
because it is good
is only right.

BAD

Is
"bad"
so bad?

ACT

Come now:
the night is whispers and smiles
and everybody knows it anyway,
so cut the act and lay it out
in the dark where everyone can see.

ANYMORE

Crickets' jagged chirps in the night
and Lao Tzu makes no sense anymore;
what's it all for
if it's not for nothing?

LEAVE

Leave me to jazz—
to Coltrane purring the moon and stars
  from his sax
and me and my Earle with much to do
and the chirps of crickets and Coltrane
into the night exploring the rhythm of
  being.

LATENIGHT

I am not sleepy or hungry or horny,
but I wish to be;
it's been a real lame night so far.

ALABAMA

Coltrane made me cry
for
four
dead
little
girls
in birmingham.

BLUES

If your throat were a harp,
your lips a trumpet,
your feet two drumsticks,
what would you say?

SPIDER

For weeks a big black spider
has been weaving its intricate web
against the corner of my bathroom
  floor,
and every night as I stand brushing my
  teeth I stare at it
and I simply haven't the heart.

FALLING

What happens
to all those little leaves
in the forest fall?

TREES

Are we so much better than
trees
all of a sudden?

WHO

I wonder if we know who trees are;
how else can we explain the way we
     treat them?

PINE

Only one pine was left
to stand in Inkster— a monument
beside the Evergreen Motel.

WHEATHER

I wonder whether
it's you or the weather
that needs to change.

BLANCHE

I've always depended
on the kindness of pussies.

LOVE(D)

She is beautiful
She is smart
She is fun
She is exciting
She is different
She is sweet
She is compassionate
She is magnificent
She is in my dreams
She is on my mind
She is in my heart
She is my love
She is my air
She is my earth
She is my light
She is my life
She is my everything
She is gone.

PASSING

She saw me passing in the park
and smiled,
but after all those years and words,
I saw her too
and I didn't dare smile back.

SUMMERGIRLS

All the pretty girls
go for the summer
to Lebanon.

NADIE

No sabes que tú eres mi
todo
y mi
nada.

RONG

Is it really so wrong
to dream about her face
and her smile and her eyes
when no one is watching?

TOUCH

What's your crazy? Give it to me
if you dare to touch it yourself.

DOWN

Why have you come?
Be on your way;
the world is coming down.

PERFECT

Something about perfection
disgusts me.

URGE

While I was
walking through
the dense wood
and I spotted a metal
fence to my left,
tall and barbed-wired,
I found myself
bewildered
by my instincts;
for hard as I tried,
I could not
fight the urge
to cross

THANK YOU

So much
for buying!
I hope you like the
book! I've also included
some stickers! If you're
happy with your
purchase, please consider
leaving a review,
Thanks!!

it.

ONCE

Aside from hard drugs and murder,
try everything once.

ONCE 2

Aside from ~~hard drugs and~~ murder,
try everything once.

KEY

Keep this key
until next year;
whatever you do,
don't give it to me sooner.

EVIL

I've always scoffed
at black cats and talismans,
evil eyes and envy and blowers in
  knots—
but every blue moon I cross a being
who makes me believe in
evil again.

CRAZY

Sometimes I wish that certain people
   were dead
And others would live forever,
That I could torture my childhood
   bullies
And redo lost fights with past lovers.
Sometimes I hate strangers on sight
And sometimes I love them.
Sometimes I talk to myself,
Sing in the shower,
Cry for no reason,
Skip washing my hands,
Squash bugs and smile,
And ogle sexy cartoon characters.
I wonder what dogs and birds are
   thinking,
Why mosquitoes bite,
Why I snot,
And why "goose" are "geese" but "moose"
   aren't "meese".
Sometimes I'm terrified but I smile
And I'm happy but I hate it.
Most times I fear or worship myself.
But craziest of all is not that I know
   I'm crazy,
But that you think you're not.

DELIVERY

I'd like to think
that I can wait weeks or days,
but I don't know who I'll be by then.

MONSTER

There is a monster in thee;
find it,
face it,
slay it,
then you will be free.

DETROIT

I miss dangerous Detroit
I miss dark Detroit
I miss angry Detroit
I miss empty Detroit
I miss scary Detroit
I miss ugly Detroit
because this Detroit that's coming back
is uglier, scarier, emptier, angrier,
    darker, and more dangerous than ever.

WISE

The old wise man
hath so much yet
to learn from the child.

SATURDA.M.

Hey Dad.
Hey Son.
It's good to see you.
It's good to see you.
I'm sorry that it's under these
  circumstances.
Can I buy you a coffee?
Sure. PLEASE.

BREAK

Sometimes you must
break your parents' hearts
for their own good.

ADVICE

Mama,
you were right
about so many things
that you are wrong about.

FATHERS

So what's the deal with
fathers
anyway?

LEARN

What can I learn
from this man's
stupidity?

206

Mama died in 206
in 204 a grown man wails
in 208 two nurses change the sheets

AGE

So what
will you do
when
age
happens to you?

RICH

I bet you can't tell me who
was the richest man in the world
the year Jesus died.

WILLOWS

Old dead drooping branches
rocking in the gales, prepared to snap;
let them.

FAME

Just let me know
when my fifteen minutes are up.

OTHER WORKS BY
YOUSEF ALQAMOUSSI

chapter one: Costa Rica
The Massacre of Heartbreak Morrow
Renegade Rebel

www.alqamoussi.com

Made in the USA
San Bernardino, CA
15 July 2019